It was a very good day to be out.
Beetle sat in the sun.
He was looking at Cricket jump
up and down.

1

Cricket jumped over to Beetle.
"Great day, isn't it?" said Cricket.

"It is, but I'm very sad," said Beetle.
"I can't jump like you.
I try, but I can't."

"You have to try, try again,"
said Cricket.
And off she went.

4

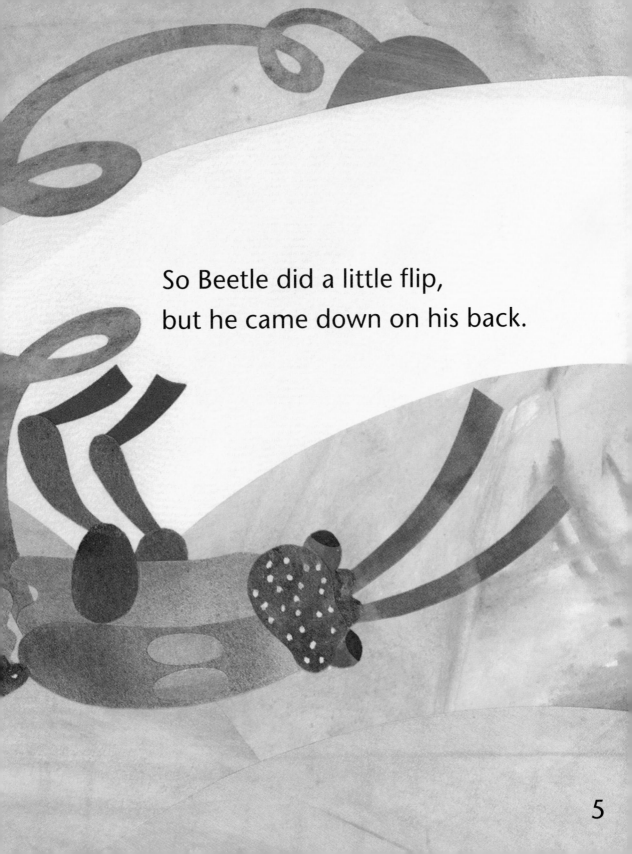

So Beetle did a little flip,
but he came down on his back.

"I have to try, try again," said Beetle.
"But I need some help.
Spider, can you help me to jump?"

"No," said Spider.
"I can spin, but I can't jump."

7

"I have to try, try again," said Beetle.
"But I need some help.
Worm, can you help me to jump?"

"No," said Worm.
"I can dig, but I can't jump."

"I have to try, try again," said Beetle.
"But there's no one here to help me."

"Don't be sad, Beetle," said Cricket.
"I'm here.
You can't jump like me,
but you can jump WITH me!"

And off they went.